MORE
FRIEND
OF
JESUS

Dedication

To all those parents, teachers and catechists
who support children on their journey of faith.

_____

Acknowledgements

I would like to thank my family, community and colleagues for their
support, encouragement and interest and especially Sister Mary
O'Gorman ra, for her proof-reading.

First published in 2003 in the United Kingdom by
McCrimmon Publishing Co. Ltd.
10-12 High Street, Great Wakering, Essex SS3 0EQ
Email: mccrimmons@dial.pipex.com
Internet: www.mccrimmons.com

© 2003 Sr Victoria Hummell ra and
McCrimmon Publishing Co. Ltd

ISBN 0 85597 650 0

Cover design: Alan Hencher and Nick Snode. Page design/layout: Nick Snode
Printed and bound in the United Kingdom by Thanet Press Ltd, Margate, Kent

Contents

Introduction

These are the stories of women and men who were friends of Jesus and helped to spread the Gospel News about him to other people. They were not perfect, but they were holy because they kept trying to follow the example of Jesus more closely. They are part of our story, the story of God's family. We can learn something from each of them.

The stories were often not written down but passed on by word of mouth. The details of the story changed and sometimes became exaggerated. The important part of the story is how much they loved God, their Creator, and wanted to be like Jesus, his Son, in his love and kindness.

1
The beginning of Christianity
The First Millennium

After Jesus returned to Heaven, His friends travelled through the nearby countries telling people the Good News about Him. They taught the people how to live in Jesus' way. Many people were baptised and became Christians. At the beginning it was difficult to be a Christian because the Roman authorities, who ruled much of the world, thought everyone should worship the Emperor, not God, so Christians like St Alban were often put to death. Gradually the Roman nation and its emperors became Christian too.

During the first thousand years after Christ, the first millennium, Christianity spread to many countries. However it was a difficult time to live in; pagans would raid Christian areas, burn down churches and take people hostage. There were many brave people who continued to be friends of Jesus in spite of the dangers. They often travelled long and dangerous distances to spread the Good News to those who had not heard it.

Alban

THE ROMAN EMPIRE was very large. The Romans controlled many countries from Palestine, where Jesus lived, to England. About two hundred and fifty years after Jesus had lived on earth there was a Roman soldier called Alban living in a town called Verulamium about 25 miles north west of London.

Diocletian, who was Emperor at that time, did not like Christians because they would not worship the Roman gods. The Romans thought that if you did not worship the pagan gods then the empire might not be strong. Diocletian had Christian churches destroyed and Christians killed. It was a difficult and dangerous time to be a follower of Jesus.

A Roman coin with the likeness of Constantine – the first Christian Emperor.

Alban was a soldier who worshipped the Roman gods. One day he met some Christians who taught him about Jesus.

No one is exactly sure of the story of St Alban, but it was something like this: Alban worshipped the Roman gods but one day he met some Christians and learnt about Jesus. He knew in his heart that following Jesus and all he taught was right, so he wanted to become a Christian. A priest visited Alban's house, taught him about Christianity and baptised him. Alban let the priest stay with him, secretly, as it was dangerous to be a priest.

One day there was a knock on his door. Some soldiers had come to arrest the priest. Alban quickly let the priest out of the back door and put on his robes and pretended he was the priest. The soldiers searched the house and arrested Alban, thinking he was the priest. He was tried before a military court, and beheaded. Alban never said who the real priest was. ➤

What do you think?

1   Why do you think that Alban wanted to become a follower of Jesus?

2   Sometimes it is hard to stick up for what you believe in. Have you ever been in that situation? What helped you?

3   What kind of special memorial or shrine would be suitable to remember Alban? Can you design one?

Alban

Alban was the first Christian in England to die for following Jesus, that is, to be a martyr. Many years later, when all the people in England were Christians, a beautiful abbey was built in the town we now call St Albans and in it there is a special memorial to remember the bravery of Alban.

Find out more

1   The Church remembers St Alban on 20th June. What would be a good hymn to sing or scripture to have on that day?

2   Find out more about the Romans. What was the name of the first Emperor to become a Christian?

3   What was the life of a Roman soldier like?

4   There were many people who died for their faith in Roman times. Can you find out more about any of them? Clue... you will find some names in the prayer sometimes said at Mass, Eucharistic Prayer I.

5   Look at a map and find where St Albans is. London or Londinium, as it was called in Roman times was about 25 miles away from St Albans. How long would it take a Roman soldier to march from one town to the other?

Link with the Bible

The greatest love a person can have for his friends is to give his life for them.   John 15: 13

Do you think these words might be suitable for Alban? Why?

Can you think of any other words from the Bible which might be appropriate?

Augustine of Canterbury

POPE GREGORY I lived in Rome about five hundred years after the time of Jesus. He was worried that the people in the south of England did not know about Jesus; they were called Anglo-Saxons. The people in other parts of Britain were Christians. Gregory decided to send his friend Augustine, who was a monk in Rome, to England to tell the people about Jesus.

When Augustine and his group of monks reached France, they heard frightening stories about the people of England. ➤

Augustine of Canterbury

Augustine had heard some frightening stories about the people of England. He told the Pope that he would rather not go there.

Augustine sent a messenger back to Pope Gregory saying he would rather not go to England, but the Pope sent the messenger back telling him to be brave and go.

When Augustine and his monks landed in Kent, King Ethelbert was friendly and even gave them a house in Canterbury. Augustine did not know that the King's wife Queen Bertha was a Christian princess. The King allowed Augustine and his monks to teach the people about Jesus. Ethelbert listened carefully and eventually he asked to be baptised. On June 2, in the year 597, Augustine baptised Ethelbert and all his family and servants. After that the Christian faith spread quickly among the Anglo-Saxons.

Augustine baptised King Ethelbert of England, his family and his servants.

Augustine was made archbishop, and put in charge of all the Christians in England. He started a monastery and a school in Canterbury. He died in 604 CE[1].

1 AD or CE, meaning *Anno Domini*, that is, 'in the year of our Lord', or 'Common Era', sometimes taken as 'Christian Era'. All three terms count the years from the birth of Jesus.

What do you think?

1   If you were Augustine what would you want to tell the people about Jesus?

2   Have you ever been frightened as Augustine was? What helped you? Did you find out that it was not as frightening as you thought?

3   What kind of a person do you think King Ethelbert was?

Find out more

1   On a map find the distance from Rome to Canterbury in Kent.
    How do you think Augustine and his monks travelled?
    How long do you think that would have taken them?

2   Can find out anything about the Cathedral at Canterbury?
    Maybe a computer would be helpful.

3   The leader of the Catholic bishops of England and Wales lives in London. Can you find where he lives, what his name is, and what his Cathedral is called?

Link with the Bible

Whoever holds out to the end will be saved.   Mark 13: 13

Do you think these words might be suitable for Augustine? Why?

Can you think of any other words from the Bible which might be appropriate?

Brigid

I RELAND HAS MANY SAINTS and holy people. Brigid is one of the three patron saints of Ireland; the other two are Patrick and Columba.

Brigid was born about 453 near Kildare in County Louth in Ireland. Her mother was a Christian slave, her father of royal blood. As a child she used to help her mother look after the cattle, to milk them, make butter and cheese.

Her mother taught her about Jesus and helped her to pray. When she was an adult Brigid asked St Patrick to baptise her.

She knew from that moment on that she wanted to give all her life to Jesus. Her father wanted to arrange a marriage for her. He knew that would be easy because Brigid was a friendly and kind person, who was also very beautiful, so lots of young men would want to marry her. However Brigid had other ideas. She did not want to marry but to give her life to prayer and helping people. Her father allowed her to do this because she won him over by her love.

Brigid's mother taught her about Jesus and helped her to pray.

Together with some friends, they went to the Bishop and made a solemn promise to give all their heart to God and not to marry. They wore a veil, a head covering, and a special robe as a sign of belonging to Jesus. Together they agreed to pray, give up comforts, to live together sharing everything and to help other people. They had a little farm with cows, chickens and vegetables.

Soon Brigid became renowned for her skill in healing people. Her mother had taught her how different herbs could heal illnesses. As well as healing the sick and the poor, Brigid also told them how much God loved them and how he had sent his son Jesus to help us. One day Brigid was sitting at the bedside of a pagan chief who was dying. As she sat there she picked up some rushes from the floor and wove them into the shape of the Cross. The chief asked her what she was doing and Brigid told him about how Jesus loved us so much he died on the Cross for us. The chief asked to be baptised. ➣

Brigid had been taught by her mother how different herbs could heal people.

Brigid

Through Brigid so many people became friends of Jesus that she is known as the Mary of the Gael (Ireland), because she brought Jesus to Ireland, a little like Mary who through his birth gave us Jesus.

What do you think?

1   Brigid was known to be prayerful, firm, humble, patient, forgiving and loving. Which three of those qualities do you like best and would like to have yourself?

2   What do you think Brigid's mother taught her about Jesus?

3   What kind of rules do you think Brigid and her friends made?

Find out more

1   The feast of St Brigid is kept on 1st February. In Ireland on that day people plait crosses of rushes which are blessed at Mass and kept in the house or the cowshed to ensure its safety. Can you find a picture of a plaited cross of St Brigid to copy?

2   What can you find out about two other important saints in Ireland, Patrick and Columba?

3   Brigid is the patron saint of farmers. Could you think of any other sort of people whom she could be the patron saint of?

Link with the Bible

Happy are those who are humble,
they will receive what God has promised.   Matthew 5: 5

Do you think these words might be suitable for Brigid? Why? Can you think of any other words from the Bible which might be appropriate to her?

Caedmon

C AEDMON LIVED IN WHITBY in Yorkshire; he looked after the cows that belonged to the Abbey at Whitby. In the evening after supper the workmen of the Abbey used to gather around the fire and sing songs. They had one small harp which they would pass around for each person to play and sing to. Caedmon had never learnt to sing; he was very embarrassed when it was getting near to his turn to sing so he would creep quietly away and hide in the cowshed. ➤

Caedmon

Caedmon had never learnt to sing; he was very embarrassed when he was asked to sing. He would creep quietly away and hide in the cowshed.

One day after he had done this he lay down in the shed and went to sleep. In his dreams he saw a man who said to him: "Caedmon, sing me something." Caedmon told him he could not sing, but the man insisted that he could. So Caedmon gave in and asked him what he would like him to sing. 'A song about the Creation of the World,' replied the man. In his dream Caedmon composed and sang a poem of praise to God for Creation. In the morning when he woke up he remembered what had happened and what he had sung.

Caedmon had a dream in which a man asked him to sing to him: In the morning when he woke up he remembered what had happened and what he had sung.

He told Hilda the Abbess of Whitby what had happened. She asked him to sing his song. This time he was not afraid and sang out loudly and clearly the song he had made up about Creation. Hilda thought it was a very beautiful song; she told him he had been given this gift by God and asked him to make up some more songs.

What do you think?

1   What do you think about Caedmon creeping away when it was his turn to sing?

2   How do you usually cope when someone asks you to do something you think is too difficult for you?

3   Which is your favourite hymn, why do you like it, what does it tell you about God?

Caedmon became a monk in Whitby Abbey and composed many more songs from Bible stories, which helped the ordinary people who could not read to understand God's message of love for them. Here is part of one Caedmon's songs:

> *The earth as yet was not green with grass:*
> *Ocean covered in eternal night*
> *Far and wide the dark ways.*
> *Then was the glory, bright spirit of heaven's Guardian,*
> *Borne over the deep sea with great speed.*
> *The Creator of angels, the Lord of Life,*
> *Light came to earth.*

Find out more

1   How do you think Caedmon felt when he discovered he could make up songs and sing them?

2   Why were songs such a good way to teach people about God in Caedmon's day?

3   Could you re-write Caedmon's song in your own words so that people today could understand it. Or could you write your own poem about a Bible story?

Link with the Bible

> *It is good to sing praise to our God:*
> *it is pleasant and right to praise him.*   Psalm 147

Do you think these words might be suitable for Caedmon? Why?

Can you think of any other words from the Bible which might be appropriate?

Cuthbert

C UTHBERT WAS BORN IN 633 AD in the north east of
England in the county we now call Northumberland. He was
a shepherd, who spent many hours on the hills protecting
his sheep from danger. This gave him time to pray and think
about God. Cuthbert was about eighteen years old when one night
when he was praying the sky lit up and he saw a picture of St Aidan
from the monastery of Lindisfarne being carried to heaven by angels.
Aidan had died that day. Cuthbert took this as a sign that God
wanted him to serve as a monk, just as Aidan had. So Cuthbert went
straight to the nearest monastery, in Melrose, and became a monk.

Cuthbert prayed a lot and tried to be a good friend of Jesus. When Cuthbert was thirty years old he was sent to Lindisfarne (sometimes called Holy Island) to help the abbot run the monastery. When the abbot was away, which was quite often, Cuthbert was in charge of the monastery. He guided the monks with gentleness but firmness. It was a difficult time because there were changes happening. The churches in the north of England were told to follow the Roman customs (*read the story of Hilda for more information*). The monks did not want to change the old ways that Aidan had taught them but Cuthbert persuaded them by his kindness.

The people in the area loved Cuthbert. They came to him with their worries and problems. He healed them so they felt better. Cuthbert wanted to spend more time alone with God just listening and talking to him. He went to live alone on an island. The animals and birds of the island were his friends; because he loved God he loved and cared for all God's creatures.

He especially loved and cared for the eider ducks who shared the island with him. They are often called Cuddy's ducks after St Cuthbert.

The people in the area came to Cuthbert with their worries and problems. He healed them so they felt better.

In 685 he was made Bishop of Lindisfarne. He did not want to leave his island and do this important job, but he knew that was what God wanted. After two years he returned to his island where he died in 687. ➤

Cuthbert

What do you think?

1 Being in the hills alone with his sheep gave Cuthbert the chance to talk to God. Do you have a special place where you like to go and be alone and talk to God?

2 People went to Cuthbert when they had problems. Whom do you go to when you are worried?

3 Cuthbert loved all God's creatures. If you could choose one animal as your friend which would it be and why?

Find out more

1 Cuthbert had to persuade the monks to change some of the things they were used to doing. What do you think is the best way to help people change? Have you ever had to do that?

2 Find Lindisfarne (Holy Island) on a map.

3 St Cuthbert was eventually buried in Durham Cathedral. See if you can find out more about this beautiful church.

4 Find a picture of eider ducks, research them and find out how the female eider cares for her young.

Link with the Bible

Jesus went all over Galilee teaching... preaching the Good News... and healing the people... Matthew 4: 23

Do you think these words might be suitable for Cuthbert? Why?

Can you think of any other words from the Bible which might be appropriate?

David of Wales

D AVID WAS BORN IN THE SIXTH CENTURY after Jesus, on a windswept headland at St Bride's Bay in Pembrokeshire in Wales. His mother was called Non, his father was the King of South Wales. His name in the Welsh language is Dewi. He went to a monastery school where he learnt to pray, to read and write and to read the Bible. He was a kind and gentle person who liked to pray and study. He became a priest and travelled around telling people about how God, our Father, sent his Son Jesus to show us his love. ➢

David of Wales

David built many churches with monasteries next door so the monks could care for the church. The monks spent their days in prayer, working in the fields, writing holy books and they gave poor people any help they might need. They lived without any luxuries; they ate bread, water and vegetables.

David made a pilgrimage, that is a holy journey, to Rome with some of his friends. He wanted to meet the Pope and to see the famous city in which the apostles spread the Good News. It was a long and difficult journey by sea, on foot and sometimes by pony. The Pope was pleased to see David; he knew he was a friend of Jesus and had been helping other people to be friends of Jesus. After David left Rome he went to Jerusalem to see the places where Jesus had lived and taught.

The Pope was pleased to see David; he knew he was a friend of Jesus.

Finally he returned to Wales, to the place where he was born. His mother Non was very pleased to see him. David built a monastery there in a place we now call St David's in West Wales. It was built in a sheltered valley where raiders who sailed past could not see it.

At this time monasteries were often raided and the monks captured or killed. The buildings were simple, small bee-hive-shaped huts made of stone, for the monks, and a bigger building for the church, all surrounded by a wall of earth and stones as protection.

David lived quietly and peacefully in his monastery until one day a messenger arrived asking him to go to a place in Wales called Brefi, where the leaders of the Church were holding a meeting (a Synod). They wanted David to talk to the leaders at this meeting and help settle an argument. David did not want to go, he thought he would not be able to help, but after he had prayed about it he knew that God wanted him to go. The leaders were so impressed by David's wisdom and holiness that his monastery was made a Cathedral and he was made an Archbishop.

David founded many churches throughout South Wales and his shrine at St David's became a special place of pilgrimage. His feast day is March 1; he is the patron saint of Wales. ➤

What do you think?

1   What did David learn at school? What would you miss of your own schooling if you went to his school instead?

2   David travelled around spreading the Good News. What Good News of Jesus would you like to tell people about?

David of Wales

Find out more

1   Look at a map of Wales and find out where Pembrokeshire is and the city of St David's. Perhaps you might find out more about the city and the cathedral on the Internet.

2   David is often pictured with a white dove on his shoulder. What do you think this tells us about David?

3   Can you imagine what life would have been like for a monk at the time of St David; what would have been important and what might you have been afraid of?

4   At the time of David all the Bibles were written out by hand by the monks using a pen and ink and parchment. They drew pictures around the page and sometimes made the capital letters at the beginning of chapters look like people or animals.
    Try writing out your own favourite verse from the Bible like this.

Link with the Bible

Jesus went all over Galilee teaching... preaching the Good News... and healing the people...   Matthew 4: 23

Do you think these words might be suitable for David? Why?

Can you think of any other words from the Bible which might be appropriate?

Hilda of Whitby

HILDA WAS BORN IN 614. Her uncle King Edwin was a very powerful ruler in the north of England. When Hilda was thirteen years old, the first Christian missionary monk came to the north of England from Canterbury. His name was Paulinus. King Edwin and his family became friends of Jesus and were all baptised. When Hilda was nineteen disaster struck. The area where she lived was invaded by another King. King Edwin was killed in battle. Hilda survived and two years later another good Christian King called Oswald ruled the land. ➤

Hilda of Whitby

When Hilda was thirty-three she realised that God wanted her to give all her life to him and she became a nun.
She was going to go to a convent in France but Aidan, the bishop of Lindisfarne, persuaded her to stay in Britain and she joined the Abbey at Hartlepool. After being there for eight years she moved to Whitby where she started a new Abbey on the hilltop over looking the sea. The abbey had a section for monks and one for nuns: Hilda was the Abbess who looked after everyone. The abbey was a happy place, the women and men loved God through their prayers and their care of the poor people in their area.

Hilda could read and write which was quite unusual in those days.

Hilda could read and write which was quite unusual in those days. She taught the monks and nuns about the Bible. Hilda encouraged a cowherd called Caedmon to sing the story of God so that everyone could hear it and understand it (*see the story of Caedmon*).
There was also a school in the abbey. Hilda was well known for being a wise and holy person; kings came to ask her advice.

At that time, long before telephones and televisions, it was not always easy to know what was going on.
The Christians in Ireland and the north of England had their own customs such as the date of Easter, which were

different from those of Rome where the Pope lived. The Pope decided it would be a good idea to have a meeting to talk about it. The meeting was called a Synod. The Abbey at Whitby was chosen as the place for the meeting because it was such an important abbey. Eventually it was decided that everyone would adopt the customs of Rome.

Hilda died in 680. She is someone people remember because she was a person who followed Jesus and helped others to know him. ➤

What do you think?

1   The nuns and monks of Whitby Abbey were happy because they loved God. Is there a special prayer you like to say or someone you help that makes you happy?

2   If you wanted to send a message to someone in another country how would you do it? How do you think the people who lived in Hilda's time would have sent messages?

3   People came to ask Hilda's advice because she was a good person. What advice do you think she might give you if you spoke to her?

Hilda of Whitby

Find out more

1   From a map find out where Whitby in Yorkshire is.

2   Can you imagine what it was like to live in the Abbey at Whitby?
    The monks and nuns probably lived in wooden buildings with
    thatched roofs. The church would have been made of stone.
    They got up early in the morning to pray and have breakfast, then
    studied or worked in the fields. Using a book or a CD-ROM look up
    the life of a nun or monk and write out a daily timetable.

3   Find out about St Aidan; clue: he came to Lindisfarne from Iona.

Link with the Bible

The disciple Paul, taught the people the word of God.

Acts 18: 11

Do you think these words might be suitable for Hilda? Why?
Can you think of any other words from the Bible which might be
appropriate?

Martin of Tours

M ARTIN WAS BORN IN THE COUNTRY we now call Hungary about three hundred years after Jesus. His father was an officer in the Roman army. When he was quite young he began to learn about Jesus and wanted to become His friend. As the son of a Roman soldier Martin had to join the Army and become a soldier.

He was sent to a place in France called Amiens. One cold night, when he was on duty guarding the barracks he found a poor man huddled under an arch shivering with cold. ➤

Martin of Tours

Martin immediately took off his own warm cloak and with one stroke of his sword cut part of it off and gave it to the beggar. The next night in his dreams he saw Jesus wearing the piece of his cloak that he had given away. He felt very close to Jesus and wanted to be a Christian so he asked a priest to baptise him. From then onwards he did everything he could to help those in need. He got

permission to leave the army because he wanted to do Jesus' work. For a while he was a hermit, living alone and spending all his time praying.

For a while Martin lived as a hermit, living alone and spending all his time praying.

Martin was well known for his love of Jesus and for his kindness and gentleness to everyone. He was chosen to be the Bishop of Tours.

As bishop, he cared for his people by travelling around his area on a donkey, or by boat, or on foot, preaching the Good News of Jesus, building churches and monasteries and caring for those in need. He brought warmth and light to hundreds of people: they thought he was like Jesus in disguise.

Martin often travelled around on a donkey preaching the Good News of Jesus.

What do you think?

1   What do you like best about Martin?

2   Why was Martin chosen as a bishop?

3   Martin was a missionary spreading the Good News about God's love for us. How can we do the same today?

Find out more

1   In France many people celebrate the feast of St Martin on 11th November by turning off the lights and walking through their house carrying lanterns and singing special songs about him.
    Can you imagine why they might do that?

2   Look up the gospel of St Matthew, chapter 25 verses 31 to 40. How does this story of Jesus describe the actions of Martin?

3   What can we learn from Martin?

4   Who is the bishop of your area, where does he live, what does he do?

Link with the Bible

Come, you who that are blessed by my Father...
I was naked and you clothed me...   Matthew 25: 34,36

Do you think these words might be suitable for Martin? Why?
Can you think of any other words from the Bible which might be appropriate?

Nicholas

NICHOLAS LIVED IN WHAT IS NOW TURKEY about three hundred years after Jesus had lived on earth.

Nicholas was a monk who gave all his time to prayer and doing good. Because everyone had heard of his holiness he was asked to be Archbishop.

There are many stories about Nicholas. One day whilst he was on a journey he stopped at an inn where the innkeeper had killed three boys. Nicholas brought the boys back to life and showed the innkeeper how bad his deeds were and how God forgives anyone who is sorry. The innkeeper became a friend of Jesus and led a good life after that.

In those days, when a girl was getting married, her father had to pay money (a dowry) to her future husband.

There was a very poor old man who could not afford to pay for his three daughters to

Nicholas showed the innkeeper how bad the things were that he had done but that God forgives anyone who is sorry. The innkeeper became a friend of Jesus and led a good life after that.

be married so he was going to sell them as slaves. Nicholas heard about this and one night when the poor man was asleep with his window open Nicholas threw a bag of gold through the window. The poor man could not believe his eyes, a bag of gold! He called his eldest daughter and told her that she could now get married because he was able to pay her dowry. A little later Nicholas came along at night with another bag of gold and threw it in the window, the second daughter was now able to be married. They all wondered where the gold had come from and would there be any for the youngest daughter?

When Nicholas came along a third time the poor man was waiting for him in the shadow of his house. As Nicholas was about to throw the third bag of gold though the window the poor man ran up to him and fell at his feet, weeping and saying how kind Nicholas was and how sorry he was that he had planned to sell his daughters.

Nicholas became well known for his love and kindness towards children and young people. ➢

What do you think?

1 What makes Nicholas such a good person?

2 Have you ever been very kind to someone secretly? What did you do? Why is it good to do that?

3 What did you notice about the innkeeper and the poor man? How did they become friends of Jesus?

Nicholas

Find out more

1   In Holland parents often give their children presents on the feast of St Nicholas, on 6th December. Can you find out any more about this custom?

2   Paintings of St Nicholas show him with a long white beard and a kindly smile. Whom might he remind you of?

3   St Nicholas is the patron saint of children and has become Santa Claus today. Can you imagine why?

Link with the Bible

Come you that are blessed by my Father...
I was hungry and you fed me,
thirsty and you gave me a drink...   Matthew 25: 34-35

Do you think these words might be suitable for Nicholas? Why?

Can you think of any other words from the Bible which might be appropriate?

2
Christianity grows
The Middle Ages

The first friends of Jesus spread the Good News so well that after the first thousand years most of the people of what we now call Europe were Christians. This was a time during which beautiful churches and cathedrals were built. Artists painted wonderful pictures of the life of Jesus and the saints to go into the churches. These pictures helped the ordinary people, most of whom could not read, to understand the stories from the Bible and the lives of saints.

Many women and men chose to follow Jesus in a special way by living in convents and monasteries, where they spent all their time in prayer, study and in helping others. Some copied out the Bible and other holy books and drew colourful pictures to illustrate them. In those days there was no other way to produce books.

This was also a time when there were many people living holy lives who later became saints. After they had died people used to go on pilgrimages to visit their tombs; this was like a holiday. They travelled together and on the way they told each other stories to pass the time.

Francis of Assisi

FRANCIS WAS BORN IN ASSISI in Italy in 1182. His father was a wealthy clothing merchant. As a young man, Francis enjoyed spending money, wearing rich clothes and living a carefree life with his friends. He dreamt of becoming a knight and of fighting battles. When he was twenty he was involved in a battle between his own town of Assisi and the nearby town of Perugia. Things did not turn out as Francis had expected and he was captured and held in prison. That gave him time to think over his life and the things that were really important. After another year his father paid the ransom money for his freedom. It took Francis a year to recover. When he was well again he soon forgot about his good thoughts.

He heard there was a war in Apulia so he got on his horse and set off. After a day of travel, he knew God was speaking to him in his heart. He turned round and went back to Assisi, where he used his wealth to help the poor, the sick and those whom no one cared for. He wore a ragged cloak and an old rope belt which he took off a scarecrow in a field and he went without shoes. His father was very angry with him and threw him out of his house. Some of his friends thought he had gone mad.

One day when Francis was at Mass he heard God tell him to leave everything behind and travel around telling people about God's love for them and to do good to everyone. Francis' love, humility and kindness attracted other young men to join him in his prayer and work. They lived very simply in wooden huts, with no chairs or tables and they slept on the ground. They made three promises called vows; to be poor like Jesus was and to share everything, to be obedient to God by following the rules they had agreed on and not to marry so they could give all their heart to God. His friend Clare wanted to live like Francis. Francis helped her gather a group of women who lived together, praying and helping the poor. ➤

Francis helped Clare gather a group of women who lived together, praying and helping the poor.

Francis of Assisi

Francis made friends with the birds and animals that lived in the woods.

Francis knew it was important to spend time alone with God, so he spent some time living in the woods on his own. While he was there he made friends with the birds and animals that lived there and thought of them as his sisters and brothers. He loved them because they were part of God's loving work of creation and he knew that all God made is very good. He made up a canticle, which is like a song, to thank God for his wonderful creation.

One Christmas Francis thought of an idea to help the poor people to understand how Jesus was born in a stable and lived like many of them, and had come on earth to show us how we could love God more. He found a cave and put a donkey and an ox in it and got some people to act out the story of the first Christmas, as Jesus, Mary, Joseph and the shepherds. The people who came to watch really understood the wonderful story of the birth of Jesus. That was the first crib.

When Francis died in 1226 he had many followers who continued to pass on God's love, and still do to this day.

What do you think?

1   It took Francis a little while to follow Jesus in the way he knew was really good. Do you ever find it difficult to do good things? What helps you?

2   What is your favourite animal? Why do you like this animal and how can you make sure it has a good life?

3   Could you make up a song, a poem or a prayer to thank God for all the wonderful creatures that we share our lives with?

4   Why was Francis' idea for a crib a really good one?

Find out more

1   Can you imagine some of the rules that Francis' first followers had? Could you think of three rules which would be very important in showing that you were a friend of Jesus?

2   The followers of St Francis are called Franciscans, the women who follow St Clare are called Poor Clares. Find out more about them. Maybe there are some living near you. You might use the Internet to help you.

3   In 1980, Pope John Paul II made Francis the patron saint of ecologists. What is an ecologist? Why is Francis such a good choice as their patron saint?

Link with the Bible

Go and preach… heal the sick… give without being paid.

Matthew 10: 8

Do you think these words might be suitable for Francis? Why?

Can you think of any other words from the Bible which might be appropriate?

Hildegard
of Bingen

HILDEGARD WAS THE LAST OF TEN CHILDREN born into a rich and noble family in Germany in 1098. In those days it was not unusual for parents who were grateful for all the blessings that God had given them to offer some of their children to God in a special way. When Hildegard was eight years old her parents gave her into the care of a holy woman called Jutta, who was a hermit (*like Julian of Norwich, in the next story*).

They lived in a hermitage near Bingen, next door to a monastery. Jutta was kind and wise, she loved Jesus and was his friend. She taught Hildegard how to pray and to read Latin; the language of the Church in those days. She taught her to read the Latin Bible and to sing the Divine Office, which is the prayer

Hildegard learnt practical skills like spinning wool.

that monks and nuns pray several times a day. Hildegard also learnet practical skills like spinning wool.

Jutta's goodness and holiness became well known and gradually more women wanted to join her so the hermitage became a Benedictine convent. When Hildegard

was fifteen years old she became a Benedictine nun and wore the black habit of that order. When Jutta died Hildegard was voted leader or abbess, she was a good and kind leader, and always looked after the sick and elderly sisters herself. Hildegard knew a lot about the healing quality of herbs and used to make medicines from them.

Hildegard wanted her convent to be a place of peace, love and harmony. Life in the convent consisted of prayer, study, art, music and manual work. ➤

Hildegard of Bingen

The day started at 2am with prayers in the chapel, then a short time in bed before morning prayer at 6am. After that there was time for study, followed by more prayers.
There was a simple breakfast, after which there was housework, then Mass, followed again by more work.
At noon there was prayer, then lunch. In the afternoon there was time for a rest until 3pm when there was prayer followed once more by work. After supper there was evening prayer, more study and the final prayer of the day. By the end of the day the nuns had prayed for three or four hours, worked for six hours and slept for eight hours. The meals were plain but healthy. They grew their own vegetables and baked their own bread.

Since Hildegard was quite young she had had visions, that is pictures of God and his love in her mind. At first she did not understand them but knew they helped her love God more. She had told Jutta but no one else. When she was older she knew she had to tell others about this experience so she wrote it down in a book called *Know the Ways of the Lord*. It took her ten years to write it.
She was not sure that it was the right thing to do, however, the Pope sent her a letter saying that he believed her visions came from God and were important.
That encouraged Hildegard. She wrote other books of poetry, music, songs, science and medicine. She wrote about creation; trees, plants and animals and how there is harmony and beauty in God's wonderful world which we must take care of.

At sixty years of age, very old for someone in those days, she felt God was asking her to go out and spread the Good News. It was not an easy thing for someone who had lived all her life in a convent. She spent several years travelling, preaching to all kinds of people, rich and poor, priests, Emperors and bishops.

When Hildegard was eighty-one she died peacefully with her community of sisters around her. Right up until that moment she had been busy telling people how much God loved them. ➢

What do you think?

1   Hildegard was always amazed at God's everlasting love in her life. Make a list of the times when you have noticed God's love in your life.

2   God wants us to take care of his creation. Is there anything you can do to take care of the earth and its creatures?

3   Hildegard wrote that the way God cares for us and carries us through life is like a feather that is carried along by the wind. When you pray can you close your eyes and imagine that God is holding you gently like a feather. How does that feel?
    What do you hear God saying to you? What do you want to say to God?

4   Jutta was a good friend to Hildegard. Who is your good friend and how does that person help you? To whom are you a good friend and how do you help them?

5   Hildegard wrote many songs which gave praise to God.
    Could you make up a song to thank God for the lovely world we live in?

Hildegard of Bingen

Find out more

1 The Divine Office, now called the Prayer of the Church, is said by priests, nuns and monks today. Find out more about it, what it mainly consists of and when it is said.

2 Hildegard was very skilled in healing sick people with herbs. Find out which herbs are used in medicine today and what they are used for, eg, peppermint for indigestion.

3 Hildegard might be considered one of the first ecologists (look at the questions for St Francis of Assisi). Why is ecology important for our future and why should it be important for a Christian?

Link with the Bible

How clearly the sky reveals God's glory...

Psalm 19

Do you think these words might be suitable for Hildegard? Why?

Can you think of any other words from the Bible which might be appropriate?

Julian of Norwich

VERY LITTLE IS KNOWN about the life of Julian of Norwich. She was probably born about 1342 in Norwich in Norfolk. She could read and write, which at that time few people, especially women, could do. She was the first woman to write a book in English. Julian was a hermit; she lived alone in a little room called a cell, attached to the church of St Julian in Norwich. It was a simple room with a bed and table and a crucifix on the plain white wall. She had a little garden where she grew vegetables and could sit and listen to the birds singing. ➤

Julian of Norwich

She spent all her time in prayer. She wanted to be very close to Jesus and try to know how he loved and how he felt, especially at the time when he died for us.
She wanted to be as close to Jesus as his Mother and friends were, when they were with him on earth.

As Julian gazed at the figure of Jesus with love, God showed himself to her in a vision.

When she was thirty years old she had a very severe illness and almost died.
The priest came to anoint her and as he left he moved the crucifix so that she could see it better. As she gazed at the figure of Jesus with love, God showed himself to her in a vision in three special ways; by what she could see, by what she could hear and by what her heart told her. God gave her some important messages in these visions which Julian wanted to share with other people.
She recovered from her illness and wrote down what had happened. The book is called *Revelation of Divine Love*, or, in other words, it is a book showing us that God is all love.

Many people heard of the visions which Julian had received and came to her hermitage in Norwich to talk to her. They came to ask for help; sometimes it is difficult to help those who are suffering. Often all Julian could do was to listen with care and reassure people that God loved them and he had given her the message in her vision that: "All will be well and all things will be well".

One of the important things Julian explained was that God is really both a Father and a Mother to us and that Jesus is our brother and like our Mother. As the cold winds from the North Sea blew across Norwich, Julian wrapped her blanket more tightly around her and thought about how God is like a warm blanket or a Mother protecting us with love and warmth, especially when life is difficult.

Julian lived at a time when there were wars and plagues and sometimes people were very cruel, but she was a happy and hopeful person because she remembered a very important thing that God had shown her in a vision. It was a little hazel-nut in the palm of her hand. God told her it was like the world, he had made it, loves it and keeps it in existence. Julian saw that she had everything she could possibly need because she was loved by God who is all goodness. ➤

What do you think?

1 Make a list of all the wonderful qualities of Mothers; then see how God is like that too.

2 Julian thought that God's love was like a warm blanket. Can you think of other ways to describe God's love?

3 If you were to visit Julian what would you like to tell her and how do you think she would reply to you?

Julian of Norwich

Find out more

1   Can you picture Julian in her hermitage? Make up a daily timetable for her.

2   Julian is called a mystic. Can you find out what that means?

3   In her writings Julian does not tell us what to do, or how to pray to become a friend of Jesus but she tells us about her own prayers and love of Jesus. Why is this a good way to encourage others to become a friend of Jesus?

4   Saints are often chosen to be patrons, for example St Cecilia is the patron saints of musicians. What would you suggest Julian be the patron of and why?

Link with the Bible

We love because God loved us first.   1 John 4: 19

Do you think these words might be suitable for Julian? Why?

Can you think of any other words from the Bible which might be appropriate?

Margaret of Scotland

MARGARET WAS A ROYAL ENGLISH WOMAN who was born in 1045 in Hungary, where her family had escaped to, when England had been invaded by the Danes. Eventually her family returned to England but were in danger again when England was invaded, this time by William the Conqueror, so she went to Scotland.

Margaret was a holy, beautiful and clever person. She often prayed and loved to read the Bible and books about saints and she was very good at embroidery. ➤

Margaret of Scotland

Malcolm, the King of Scotland, loved Margaret and wanted to marry her. He was a rough man, he could not read or write and his manners were not very good. Margaret saw the goodness in Malcolm and knew that if she showed him love and encouragement she could help him. They got married and were very happy; Margaret was now Queen of Scotland.

Margaret was very good at embroidery.

Margaret was a good influence over Malcolm.

She was a strong-willed person who had a very good influence over Malcolm. Soon the royal court in Scotland improved, and everyone was more kind and thoughtful. Many churches were built including a beautiful Cathedral in Dunfermline. Margaret persuaded Malcolm to release his slaves, to stop fighting and settle arguments in a peaceful way. He did all this because he loved Margaret.

Prayer was very important to Margaret; she knew it was important to listen to God speaking in her heart and to be a good friend of Jesus in all she thought and did. People used to notice how happy she was when she prayed. She knew that Jesus cared for poor people, Margaret loved them too and gave them food and clothes.

Malcolm and Margaret had eight children. They were good parents and loved their children. David, their son, became King after his Father had died; he was one of the kindest and best kings of Scotland.

What do you think?

1   What do you think Malcolm liked about Margaret?

2   Why do you think that Margaret was so happy when she prayed?

3   How do love and encouragement help you? Have you ever changed because of someone's good influence on you?

Find out more

1   Margaret's book of the gospels is in the Bodleian library at Oxford university; can you find out more about this library?
    How would books have been produced in Margaret's day?

2   See if you can find a picture of an illuminated manuscript.
    Try writing your name like that.

3   Why do you think that David was a good king?

Link with the Bible

Happy are those who work for peace,
God will call them his children...   Matthew 5: 9

Do you think these words might be applied to Margaret? Why?

Can you think of any other words from the Bible which might be appropriate?

Thomas of Canterbury

THOMAS WAS BORN IN LONDON on 1118, the son of a
wealthy merchant. Thomas had a good education, he was
a clever person, very reliable but he also wanted to be
important. He got a job with Theobald, a relation of his,
who was the Archbishop of Canterbury. He enjoyed travelling
around with the Archbishop to foreign countries and meeting
powerful people.

When Henry II became the new king he chose Thomas as his Chancellor. It was one of the most important jobs in England. He advised the king and helped him rule the country. They were great friends. Henry relied on Thomas and found him very useful: he rewarded him with riches. Thomas dressed richly, lived in a beautiful house, with servants and expensive furnishings. He loved to go hunting and hawking on one of his many horses. He often gave big parties for his friends and people he wanted to impress. He was probably one of the richest people in England.

When Theobald died Henry asked Thomas to be Archbishop of Canterbury. At first Thomas laughed and thought that Henry was joking. The monks at Canterbury were not very pleased at the idea, because they thought Thomas was an ambitious man and not very holy. Thomas eventually agreed. He became a priest, then Archbishop of Canterbury the next day. Henry was pleased because he thought that Thomas would do as he told him and he could get some money out of the Church by putting up their taxes.

Thomas agreed to be the Archbishop of Canterbury.

Thomas surprised and annoyed Henry when he told him he no longer wanted to be Chancellor. Something very special had happened to Thomas, he suddenly saw what was ➤

Thomas of Canterbury

important in life, it was not being rich and powerful but being a friend of Jesus, by giving time to prayer and to care for God's church, to obeying the Pope first before the King. Henry became more and more angry with Thomas when he realised he could not make him do what he wanted. In fear of his life Thomas had to escape to a monastery in France, where he stayed for six years. Eventually Thomas returned to England. Henry was still cross with Thomas and one day when some of his knights

heard the King complaining they thought they would please him if they killed Thomas. They found Thomas in the Cathedral at Canterbury and killed him there.

News of the murder spread rapidly. Henry was very sorry when he heard what had happened. People went to Canterbury on pilgrimage to pray

Some knights heard the King complaining about Thomas and made plans to kill him.

at the place where Thomas had been killed and to see his tomb in the Cathedral. Many people said that Thomas had cured them.

What do you think?

1   What kind of person was Thomas before he became the Archbishop of Canterbury. Why did he change?

2   What do you think are the most important things in life?

3   What do you think was the reason for Henry's quarrel with Thomas?

4   If you could choose to go to a Holy place where would you go and why?

 ## Find out more

1   There is a very famous poem written by Geoffrey Chaucer called *The Canterbury Tales*. It is about the stories that some pilgrims tell as they journey to Canterbury. See if you can find out anything about the stories from a book, CD-ROM or the Internet.

2   The pilgrims used to buy badges to sew onto their clothes to show they had been on pilgrimage. What badge would you design for a visitor to St Thomas of Canterbury?

 ## Link with the Bible

You will be arrested... you will be beaten... you will stand before rulers and kings for my sake to tell them the Good News...   Mark 13: 9

Do you think these words might be suitable for Thomas? Why?

Can you think of any other words from the Bible which might be appropriate?

3
Difficult times

By 1500 people were becoming more educated, the invention of printing meant that there were many more books available and they were not so expensive. This was a time of change in the world, people were beginning to have new ideas about what it meant to be a follower of Jesus, there were many arguments about religion. Sometimes when this happens it is easy to forget what is really important.

It was still a time when powerful people could bully others and try to make them do as they wished. In England Henry VIII was king and he was used to having his own way. When he wanted to divorce his wife, Catherine of Aragon, and marry Anne Boleyn he tried to get the Pope to give him permission to do so. Henry got tired of waiting for an answer so he went ahead and married Anne and called himself the Head of the Church. Many good people could not accept what Henry had done. It got worse; Henry closed down the monasteries and convents and took their money and buildings for himself and his friends.

This was a time when many good people, both Catholics and other Christians, were put to death for what they believed in; they were martyrs. Nowadays Christians talk to and try to understand each other and to pray together that one day all Christians may be united. The word for this is ecumenism.

In other parts of the world where Francis Xavier and Martin de Porres were born there were no changes in the religion of the country like those in England.

Francis Xavier

F RANCIS WAS BORN INTO A RICH FAMILY in Spain in 1506.
He was a clever boy so he was sent to the University of
Paris to study. While he was in Paris he met a student called
Ignatius from Loyola. Francis told him how he wanted to be
a rich and famous soldier and maybe work for the king.

Ignatius asked him whether he would think of becoming a soldier
for Jesus. He thought that Francis was a good and cheerful young
man who would make an excellent companion of Jesus, so he

invited Francis to join the group he was starting called the Company of Jesus.

These men prayed and also preached the Good News of the Gospel wherever the Pope thought people needed to hear that message.
Francis knew this was what he really wanted to do too, so in 1534 in the church of St Peter in Montmartre in Paris Francis joined Ignatius and five others and took vows or special promises to follow Jesus. Three years later they were all ordained priests.

While Francis was in Paris he met a student called Ignatius from Loyola.

Francis knew he had to take the Good News of Jesus to all those people who had not heard it; he was a missionary. First of all he set sail from Portugal for Goa in India. His journey by sailing ship was long and dangerous. It took thirteen months and was hard for Francis because he suffered from seasickness. When he arrived he lost no time in telling everyone about how much God loved them and how he sent his Son Jesus to show us how to live. To help the people remember what he had taught them he made his teaching into songs using popular tunes.

He lived very poorly, sleeping on the ground in a hut and eating mainly rice and water. It was the poor who listened most to Francis and became followers of Jesus. For the next few years he worked among the people of south India and Sri Lanka. He even went to Japan. Francis wrote to Ignatius very often. In one his letters he told him that there were lots of people wanting to hear about Jesus and he wished that all those clever people at the University in Paris would love Jesus more than their books and come and help him. ➤

Francis Xavier

Francis dreamed of taking the Good News to the people of China. It was quite difficult to get into the country as they did not allow foreigners in. On the way there he got very

ill so the ship he was on stopped at an island and dropped him off. From there he could see China and he prayed for the people of China but he did not get there. He died on the island.

On the way to China, Francis became very ill.

What do you think?

1   Ignatius made a difference to Francis' life when he persuaded him to join his group. Who is the person who helps you make good choices in your life?

2   Francis had a very good way of teaching people about Jesus by using song tunes. Could you think of one or two sentences you would like to use to tell people about Jesus. What tune could you use?

3   Why do you think it was poor people who listened most to Francis?

4   Francis was a great missionary. There are many missionaries throughout the world. How could you be a missionary at home without going to a foreign country?

Find out more

1   To find out more about those special promises or vows that the Company of Jesus took, read the story of St Francis of Assisi.

2   The Company of Jesus still exists today. They are called Jesuits. They carry on the work that Ignatius started throughout the world. See if you can find out more about them from the Internet.

3   What do you think about Francis' letter to Ignatius? Would it have been a good idea for the students of Paris to leave their studies and go to India to help Francis?

Link with the Bible

Go throughout the whole world and preach the gospel to all people...   Mark 16: 15

Do you think these words might apply to Francis? Why?

Can you think of any other words from the Bible which might be appropriate?

Margaret Clitherow

MARGARET LIVED IN YORK in the reign of Queen Elizabeth I. She was brought up as a Protestant, and was an attractive, clever girl with a good sense of humour. When she was fifteen she fell in love with and married John Clitherow, a prosperous butcher. He was a kind and easygoing man. They lived over their butcher's shop in a street called the Shambles. Margaret used to help John in the shop.

After she had been married three years Margaret became a Catholic. It was a dangerous thing to do because it was against the law. Her husband, although he did not agree with her, loved her and supported her.

Margaret was sent to prison for two years for not attending the Protestant church services. Whilst she was in prison she learnt to read and write so that when she came out she

Margaret fell in love with John, a prosperous butcher. They lived over their butcher's shop in a street called the Shambles.

set up a school in her house for local Catholic children, where she taught them their faith and to read and write. Catholic priests who were being hunted by the authorities would come to Margaret who had a special hiding hole in her house where they would not be discovered. Margaret was very happy to be able to help these priests. They used to travel around the country in disguise, celebrating Mass for those who wanted to keep their Catholic faith. They often celebrated Mass secretly in Margaret's house too. Margaret kept vestments and a chalice well hidden.

The laws against Catholics became more harsh and the authorities were determined that Catholicism should be stamped out in Yorkshire where it was especially strong. When Margaret's house was raided no trace of the priests was found. Her children were very good and never gave anything away even when they were roughly questioned and threatened, neither did her servants. Eventually a Flemish boy who was a guest in the house became frightened and told the raiders where the secret hiding place was. ➤

Margaret Clitherow

Margaret was arrested, imprisoned and sentenced to death in 1586. John, her husband, was very upset; he would have given anything to free her. Margaret was an ordinary mother and housewife who was such a faithful follower of Jesus that no matter what happened she would never give up her friendship with Him.

What do you think?

1   What kind of person was John Clitherow?

2   Jesus tells us in the gospels that being a friend of his might be difficult. What difficult choices do you have to make?

3   What helps you stay a faithful friend of Jesus?

Find out more

1   Find out who was on the throne in 1586, and something about the difficulties that Catholics had in practising their faith.

2   Can you imagine what Margaret taught the children who came to her school? Make up a list of subjects. What do you learn about now, that they would not have learnt?

3   Nowadays Christians of different groups are friendly with each other and try to understand each other and pray together.
    Can you make up a prayer for the unity of Christians?
    Look up the word Ecumenism.

 ## Link with the Bible

Happy are you when people... persecute you... because you are my followers... a great reward is kept for you in heaven.

Matthew 5: 11

Do you think these words might be suitable for Margaret? Why?

Can you think of any other words from the Bible which might be appropriate?

Martin de Porres

MARTIN WAS BORN IN LIMA IN PERU in 1579. His mother was a black woman who had once been a slave. His father was a Spanish nobleman who had left Martin's mother to bring him up all by herself. In order to earn enough to feed herself and Martin she had to work hard doing washing for people. They lived in a very poor house. Martin did not have toys or new clothes, but he was a happy and generous boy. It made him sad to see the beggars in the street who were even poorer than himself. His mother was cross with him when he gave them her hard-earned money.

When Martin was eight years old he was adopted by a Spanish man living in Lima. He saw what a good, kind boy Martin was and wanted to help him. He sent him to school to learn to read and write. Martin learnt that Jesus loved the sick and poor people. Martin wanted to do the same, so he trained as a barber-surgeon; what we would now call a doctor, so that he could help people.

Martin's mother had to work hard doing washing for other people in order to earn enough money to feed themselves. They lived in a very poor house.

Martin worked in the friary hospital caring for the sick. He was gentle and kind and everyone loved him.

Martin wanted to give all his time to being a friend of Jesus, to pray and help others, so he become a brother in the Dominican Friary. He worked in the friary hospital caring for the sick. He was gentle and kind; everyone loved him and often asked his advice because they knew he was a good friend of Jesus. As he walked through the city visiting the sick he would pray the prayers of the rosary which hung from his belt.

He was very worried about the number of children who had no parents and were sleeping in the streets of Lima. He remembered these children as he prayed. Martin asked the Friar in charge if he could help them. Martin was delighted and thanked God when he was given a house where the children could live and be looked after. Martin was well known and loved by a lot of people, some of whom were rich. He told the rich people about those who were poor and they gave him money to help them. ➤

Martin de Porres

When there was a plague in the city, a very infectious disease, Martin did not worry about catching it. He thought only of the poor sick people and he visited them in their homes and brought them medicine and food.

Martin was loved by everyone for his holiness. It was easy to see how much he loved God and wanted to follow him.

What do you think?

1   Life must have been quite hard for Martin when he was young, especially as his mother had been a slave. What do you think helped Martin to be happy and cheerful?

2   Can you imagine what life was like in the house that Martin got for the homeless children? What do you think that the children would do?

3   What would the world be like if everyone was like Martin de Porres?

Find out more

1   Martin joined the Dominican order. Find out about St Dominic; when did he live, what kind of religious dress or habit do Dominicans wear, is there a Dominican friary near you?

2   Find out what barber-surgeons did in the sixteenth century. What medicines did they have? Did they ever perform operations?

3   Find out where Peru is. Why did the Spanish go there?

4   Are there homeless people in our country? How can we help them? Find out about the *Big Issue* magazine.

Link with the Bible

*I was sick and you took care of me... whenever you did
this for one of these poor ones you did it for me...*

Matthew 25: 36,40

Do you think these words might apply to Martin? Why?

Can you think of any other words from the Bible which might be
appropriate?

Nicholas Owen

ICHOLAS lived at about the same time as Margaret Clitherow; he was born in 1550. His family, who lived in Oxfordshire, had always been Catholic even though it was dangerous. It was against the law to go to Mass. Two of Nicholas's brothers became priests and a third brother secretly printed Catholic books. Nicholas became a carpenter like his father.

For a little while Nicholas gave up carpentry and acted as a servant to Fr Edmund Campion; a brave Jesuit (remember the story of Francis Xavier) priest. He travelled around the country celebrating the Mass and the other sacraments for Catholics who were trying to practice their Faith. Nicholas helped Fr Edmund change his disguise when he was being followed. Eventually Fr Edmund was captured and executed at Tyburn in London.

During the time that Nicholas had been with Fr Edmund he realised that many of the hiding holes in houses that priests used were badly built, had no ventilation and could easily be discovered. In fact many priests had been captured because of this. Nicholas thought he could use his skills as a carpenter to build safer hiding holes.

He used to be invited to a Catholic house as an ordinary workman and during the day he could be seen sawing and hammering, repairing furniture or doors. At night when all the servants were in bed he would start work on a secret hiding hole. First of all he would kneel down and spend some time praying, asking God to guide him to build a safe place. Sometimes the hole would be in a wall behind panelling or sometimes under the floor. It was hard and difficult work, which he did on his own. He never made any two holes in the same way for fear that the discovery of one might lead to the discovery of others. Sometimes Nicholas made one hole inside another so that when the first hole was discovered empty no one would look any further. In some holes he made a tube where food could be put down if the search for priests went on for a long time.

Nicholas was invited to a Catholic house as an ordinary workman and during the day he could be seen sawing and hammering, repairing furniture or doors.

Nicholas was a courageous and holy man. He was prepared to give up everything to follow Jesus. He became a brother in the Jesuits, but secretly for fear of the authorities. The first time he was captured and tortured his friends managed to bribe the prison authorities to ➢

Nicholas Owen

let him go. He had not given away any of his secrets so the authorities were fooled into thinking he was of no importance. Little did they know.

The work of Nicholas Owen saved the lives of many priests and the families of those who hid them. It ensured that Catholics could continue to practice their faith in spite of the cruel laws of that time.

Finally Owen was captured, with two priests and another brother. One hundred armed men surrounded Hindlip Hall. Nicholas and Ralph, the other brother, made sure the priests were well hidden before hiding themselves. They had no time to take anything with them but one apple. For seven days the soldiers tore the house apart but could find nothing. Nicholas and Ralph gave themselves up, pretending to be priests, hoping the soldiers would capture them and go away. But they knew they were not priests and eventually they found the priests. Nicholas was taken to the Tower of London in 1606 where he was tortured until he died, but he gave nothing away.

What do you think?

1 What do you like best about Nicholas?

2 Nicholas used his gift of carpentry. What are your gifts?
   How can you use some of your gifts to help others?

3 Nicholas was named as a saint and a martyr by Pope Paul VI in
   1970. What is a martyr? Why does Nicholas deserve to be a saint?

Find out more

1 It is difficult to appreciate what it was like to be imprisoned for going
   to Mass. How would you feel if you had been Nicholas?
   What gave him courage? Can you make up a prayer asking God to
   give you courage?

2 Find out about Tyburn. It is near what we now call Marble Arch in
   London. Quite close is a convent where the sisters remember the
   martyrs who died for their faith. You can find out more about them
   by visiting the web site of Tyburn Convent.

3 There are forty martyrs whose feast is celebrated every year on 25th
   October. Can you find out about a few of the others?

4 What can we learn about the importance of freedom from the story
   of Nicholas Owen? Could you make up a prayer about that?

Link with the Bible

*The greatest love a person can have for his friends is to
give his life for them...*   John 15: 13

Do you think these words might be suitable for Nicholas? Why?

Can you think of any other words from the Bible which might be
appropriate?

Thomas More

W HEN THOMAS WAS A YOUNG MAN in London studying
to be a lawyer he lived with the Carthusian monks.
It was a life that involved a great deal of prayer.
Thomas enjoyed having the opportunity to follow Jesus
in this way but he knew that God was asking him to live a different
kind of life. Thomas became a lawyer. He was well known for his
cleverness, hard work and honesty. Everyone knew Thomas was a
person who was fair and just. When he was only twenty-six years old
he was chosen to be a Member of Parliament for the City of London.
He was very good at discussing and winning arguments.

Thomas married and had children but sadly his wife died only five years later. Thomas married again. Thomas worked hard but he still found time to pray. He used to pray and work from 2am to 7am, then begin his working day. Family life was important for Thomas; he spent time with his children and made sure that they had a good education, girls as well as boys, which was unusual in those days.

Thomas spent time with his children and made sure that they had a good education.

Thomas was thirty-one years old when Henry VIII became King of England. Thomas was pleased because Henry's reign promised to be a good one. Henry was a friendly, clever person. Soon Henry heard of Thomas' reputation as under-sheriff in the city of London and invited him to become one of his Councillors. This was a very important job, Thomas carried out the King's business and they became good friends. Sometimes Henry would go to Thomas' house in Chelsea for dinner, and afterwards relax by walking in the garden with Thomas, chatting and laughing together. Henry knew Thomas was someone he could trust.

King Henry who was married to Catherine of Aragon had a daughter but no sons. He very much wanted a son so he could be king after him. Meanwhile Henry had become very friendly with a young woman called Anne Boleyn and wanted to marry her and divorce Catherine. Henry sent his Chancellor, Cardinal Wolsey, to see the Pope about it. The Pope would not give Henry permission to marry Anne. Henry was very cross and got rid of the Chancellor. He called Thomas in and asked him if he would be Chancellor; he thought that Thomas would do exactly what he wanted. This was a very great honour; the Chancellor was one of the most important jobs in the country. It would make Thomas rich and famous. ➤

The King would go to Thomas' house for dinner, and afterwards they would relax by walking in the garden.

Thomas More

Thomas told Henry he did not want the job. Henry got very angry and banged the table with his fist and told Thomas he did not have a choice; he had to be Chancellor.

Thomas was a good Chancellor. He carried out his work well, he listened to the concerns of everyone whether they were rich or poor and gave them justice. He tried not to get into any discussion about the King's divorce.

Henry married Anne Boleyn in 1533. Thomas was very sad at the way Catherine of Aragon had been treated and how Henry had gone against the teaching of Jesus. Henry had an Act passed by Parliament to say that any children he and Anne had would be entitled to be king or queen.
Just to be sure Henry decided that everyone should sign an Oath saying they agreed with the Act. Thomas was asked to sign it. Thomas went home and prayed about it. If he did not sign the Oath he and his family might be in very great danger, but if he did sign it when he knew it was wrong he would be going against his conscience and his love of God. He knew what he had to do, he must not sign it.

People tried to persuade Thomas to sign, but he was strong and he refused. Thomas was sent to the Tower of London and imprisoned there for over a year. Whilst he was there he missed his family but he spent his time in prayer and remembered how he had enjoyed the time he had lived with the monks. Eventually he was beheaded in 1535.
As he was about to die he said, "I die as the King's good servant, but God's first."

What do you think?

1   What do you like most about Thomas?

2   How do you know when you are doing what is right?

3   What do you think Thomas meant when he said, "I die as the King's good servant, but God's first."?

Find out more

1   Find out about the Carthusian monks. Do they have monasteries today in Great Britain? What is their daily life like? Clue: they may have a web site.

2   What does a Chancellor do?

3   Thomas More was made a saint in 1935; his special day is 22nd June. See if you can find out what reading and prayers are used on that day.

4   Thomas wrote a book called *Utopia*, it was about an ideal society. What would your ideal world be like?

Link with the Bible

You will be handed over and put to death for my sake...
but whoever holds out to the end will be saved.

Mark 13: 9,12,13

Do you think these words might be suitable for Thomas? Why?

Can you think of any other words from the Bible which might be appropriate?

4

More recent times

The nineteenth century, that is starting at around 1800, was a time when the Catholic Church in England was recovering from the harsh laws which stopped people from practising their faith.

It was a time when there were many inventions. New sources of energy were found, machines were powered by steam, using coal.
These inventions meant that such things as cotton and wool could be woven quickly and cheaply in factories instead of at home by hand on a loom. More coal was needed so more miners were needed to dig it out. The first trains were invented, they too used coal for power. New ways were found to farm so that not so many people were needed in the fields. This was a time when people moved from the country to the town. Life was changing. There was more opportunity for children to have some education. But there were still quite a lot of poor people whom few cared about.

It was a time when some people thought they could do without God. At the same time there were some people who were very close to God and were friends of Jesus.

John Bosco

J OHN BOSCO knew what it was like to be very poor. He was born in a village in Northern Italy in 1815, the youngest son of a farmer who died when John was only two years old.

His mother, Margaret, did her best to bring him up. There was very little money but lots of love.

John learnt about Jesus and would pray as he helped his mother in the fields.

One night John had a very vivid dream telling him that he had the gifts to be ➤

John Bosco

One night John had a vivid dream telling him that he had the gifts to be able to help the poor and neglected children who lived on the streets.

able to befriend the poor and neglected children who lived on the streets. When John woke up he remembered his dream; it was to change his life. He decided he would become a priest, so that he could help others become friends of Jesus. Studying to become a priest was very hard, there was a lot to learn. Eventually when he was twenty-six years old John was ordained a priest. In Italy, priests are called Don followed by their family name, so John Bosco became Don Bosco.

As a priest Don Bosco visited the streets, slums and prisons of Turin in northern Italy. He was shocked to find so many young people there who had been abandoned, no one cared for them or helped them and they were hungry. He remembered his dream and knew he had to do something for them. Don Bosco knew that education would help these young people. He believed in them and knew that Jesus loved each one of them. He started schools where the young people could learn the Christian way of living and do jobs like printing, bookbinding and shoemaking so they could earn their own living.
Don Bosco was a good leader.
The young people loved him. He learnt to do a magic balancing trick that caught their attention. They gladly listened when he taught them and liked to pray with him.

On Sundays Don Bosco would often take the young people into the country to enjoy the fresh air and beauty of nature. They would start with Mass followed by breakfast, games, a picnic, listen to some stories about Jesus and pray together before returning to the city.

Other men could see the wonderful work that Don Bosco was doing and wanted to join him. They formed a group called the Salesians, who prayed and lived together and helped care for and teach young people about the Good News of God's love for them. Some of the young people were difficult and badly behaved. Don Bosco told his followers that they were to be patient and gentle with their pupils, to love them as Jesus loved his friends and never to get angry with them.

When Don Bosco died in 1888 thousands of people lined the street as his funeral procession went by. He was loved very much by everyone. The religious order he founded continues his work today with kindness and love for young people who are poor, wherever they may be. ➢

What do you think?

1   John followed his dream. Do you have a dream you would like to follow? How might you do that?

2   Why was John so concerned about the young people of Turin?

3   What do you like most about John Bosco?

John Bosco

Find out more

1   John Bosco called his order after St Francis de Sales (Salesians). Francis was a gentle priest who said that "more flies are attracted by honey than by vinegar". What do you think that means? How did John Bosco practice that?

2   Find out more about the Salesians from their web site. They have other saints in their Order, find out about them too.

3   Who do you think are the young people most in need of help in our world today?

Link with the Bible

Let the children come to me... because the Kingdom of Heaven belongs to them.   Mark 10: 14

Do you think these words might be suitable for Don Bosco? Why?

Can you think of any other words from the Bible which might be appropriate?

Marie Eugenie Milleret

ANNE EUGENIE MILLERET was born in France in 1817. She lived in a large house in the country. She and her brother enjoyed playing in the woods and fields and looking after their pets; they even had a pet deer who ate out of their hands. Sometimes Anne Eugenie would go with her mother to visit the sick and poor people in the area and take ➤

Marie Eugenie Milleret

them food and warm clothing. She never forgot her visits to the poor and all her life had a special love for them.

When Anne Eugenie was twelve years old the day came for her to make her First Holy Communion. She was very happy at the thought of receiving Jesus for the first time. After receiving Communion, as she walked back through the crowded church, she wondered whether she would find her mother again. She heard Jesus speak to her in her heart telling her,

"I will be more than a mother to you. One day you will leave everyone in order to serve me and make me loved."

At first Anne Eugenie did not understand the meaning of this, but she remembered it all her life.

When Anne Eugenie was eighteen, living with some relations in Paris, she went to the beautiful cathedral of Notre Dame. There she heard a talk, which helped her to understand how much God loved her and it made her want to give her whole life to God. A little later she talked to a priest about this. He wanted to start a new religious order of nuns and asked her if she would begin it. Anne Eugenie was surprised and a bit scared, she told him that she knew nothing about being a nun. She prayed about this, asking God to guide her. She went to stay with some sisters and learn about their life.

Eventually at the age of twenty-two Anne Eugenie began a
new order called the Religious of The Assumption.
She started it with two others in a small flat in Paris.
They prayed, studied and lived together. They were
prepared to make three very special promises, or vows; to
be poor like Jesus and to share everything, to be obedient
to God and not to marry so they could give all their heart
to God. They wore a special dress called a habit. It was
purple to remind them of penance and giving up
everything to show their love for Jesus. They wore a white
veil to remind them of Our Lady. The sisters took new
names, Anne Eugenie changed her name to Marie Eugenie
because she loved Mary. Marie Eugenie remembered the
words Jesus spoke to her in her heart after her first Holy
Communion and knew how she would love and serve
Jesus.

The sisters opened a school for girls. In those days girls
did not usually receive a very good education.
Marie Eugenie changed that. The girls were taught
religious education, maths, science and language as well
as art and PE. Marie Eugenie wanted these girls to be
friends of Jesus and tell others about him, especially their
own children when they were mothers. The girls were also
encouraged to visit poor people as Marie Eugenie had
when she was young and to share with them.

Many women joined the Assumption sisters and spread
Jesus' message of love throughout the world and still do
so today. ➣

———————————————

Marie Eugenie Milleret

What do you think?

1   Has anyone ever asked you to do something you thought was quite difficult ? How did you feel ? What helped you?

2   Can you imagine what life was like for the first sisters?
    Could you make up a timetable for them of prayer, teaching and being together?

3   If you were a parent, how would you bring up your children to become friends of Jesus?

4   Think about the three vows or promises that the sisters made. Which one do you like best and why?

Find out more

1   What does the colour purple mean and when does the Church use it?

2   Can can find out more about the Assumption sisters today?
    Try looking on the Internet; clue; look up "assumption, religious".

3   Find out about the Assumption of Our Lady into Heaven; clue; it is one of the mysteries of the Rosary and the feast day marking it is 15th August.

Link with the Bible

Jesus replied, "Love the Lord your God with all your heart... and love your neighbour as yourself.

Mark 12: 30-31

Do you think these words might be suitable for Marie Eugenie? Why?

Can you think of any other words from the Bible which might be appropriate?

Bernadette Soubirous

ERNADETTE SOUBIROUS was born in 1844 in Southern France in a small town called Lourdes, tucked into the foot of the Pyrenees mountains. Her father was a miller, she was the eldest of six children. Her family were very poor, Bernadette had no education, she could not read or write. She was often ill so her Mother sent her to live with a friend nearby in Bartres where Bernadette helped to look after the sheep.

When Bernadette was fourteen she returned to live in Lourdes and began to prepare to make her First Holy Communion. ➣

Bernadette Soubirous

Whilst she was at home she tried to help her family. One day when she was out with her sister and a friend collecting wood for the fire at home, she heard the sound of the wind blowing strongly and as she looked around she saw a lady standing in a hollow at the top of some steep rocks. Bernadette rubbed her eyes. She thought she was imagining something. The lady had a white dress with a blue sash and was saying the rosary. Bernadette just knelt down and said the rosary too. After that the lady disappeared. The others who were with her did not see the lady. Bernadette told her mother about what had happened. A few days later she persuaded her mother to let her go again with some friends. The lady was there again, smiling at her.

News went round the town and next time Bernadette went to see the lady lots of people followed her. The lady asked Bernadette to return often. The lady spoke to Bernadette

and told her to pray. One day the lady asked her to tell the priests that people should come in procession to this spot and that eventually a chapel would be built there. The lady asked Bernadette to drink at the spring but there was no spring. Bernadette scraped away the earth near her feet and at last pure clean water came out. Some people laughed at Bernadette and tried to get her to say that she had made it all up. Bernadette was sure of what she had seen.

Bernadette scraped away the earth near her feet and at last pure clean water came out.

The priests asked Bernadette to find out the lady's name. After Bernadette had asked her her name many times the lady said, 'I am the Immaculate Conception.' Bernadette repeated this strange name to the priest. It was a name that Bernadette had never heard before, she did not know what it meant. The priest told the bishop, who now understood it was Our Lady herself who had appeared to Bernadette.

Bernadette joined the Sisters of Nevers. She often thought about all the things that Our Lady had said to her. A church was built where Our Lady had appeared and people came from all over the world – to join in the torchlight procession, to pray and bathe in the waters of the spring. Bernadette was

People came from all over the world to pray and bathe in the waters of the spring at Lourdes.

pleased that so many people were becoming better friends of Jesus by praying at Lourdes. Bernadette died aged thirty-five. ➤

What do you think?

1　Bernadette did not receive much education when she was young, but what kind of things was she good at?

2　Has anyone ever laughed at you when you have tried to explain something you believed in? What is the best thing to do if that happens?

3　Some people have been cured of their illness at Lourdes, but most people find that Lourdes gives them something else. How do you think Lourdes could help a pilgrim?

Bernadette Soubirous

Find out more

1   Our Lady said she was the Immaculate Conception.
    This means that Mary was born full of grace and goodness.
    Can you think of any time in her life when she especially showed
    her holiness?

2   Find out more about Lourdes, either from someone who has been
    there or from a web site about Lourdes.

3   Look in a hymn book and choose the hymns you would like to sing
    if you were in the torchlight procession at Lourdes.

Link with the Bible

*Jesus said, "Lord of heaven and earth, I thank you
because you have shown to the unlearned what you
have hidden from the wise and learned."*

Matthew 11: 25

Do you think these words might be suitable for Bernadette? Why?

Can you think of any other words from the Bible which might be
appropriate?

Josephine Bakhita

A S A CHILD Josephine lived in what is now the Sudan near the north of Africa. She was born about 1869. Her family were happy and loving. Her father was an important landowner. Josephine knew nothing about God but when she looked at the beauty of nature, at the sun, moon and stars she wondered who had made it.

One day when Josephine was about seven years old she was out walking in the fields with a friend when some men captured her. She was so frightened she could not scream or speak. ➤

Josephine Bakhita

They made her walk barefooted with them day and night for miles. They decided to call her Bakhita, which means 'lucky'. When they reached the men's village she was shut in a cupboard for many weeks. During that time she thought a lot about her family and would cry herself to sleep. One morning she was taken out of the cupboard and put with seven other slaves who had been captured and together they were marched to the slave market in another village. Bakhita and another girl managed to escape and run away only to be captured by another slave trader.

Bakhita was bought and sold several times by people who wanted slaves. Her life was hard and she was often treated with great cruelty. Eventually an Italian man who was working in the Sudan bought her. Bakhita was much happier; now she was well treated and was not beaten.

Her master took her to Italy where he gave her to his friend to help his wife look after their baby. The family were preparing to go to Africa. They went there for a few months, leaving Bakhita in Italy with the baby until they were quite ready. Bakhita stayed with the baby in a convent. Whilst she was there the sisters told her about Jesus and his great love for everyone. Bakhita was very happy and knew she wanted to become a friend of Jesus. She spent a lot of time talking to Jesus in prayer.

Eventually Maria, the baby's mother, returned to take Bakhita and her baby to Africa. Bakhita refused to go because she wanted to finish her preparation for baptism.

Never in her life had Bakhita ever refused to do as she was told. Maria was furious and tried her best to make Bakhita change her mind. Bakhita stayed and was baptised and made her First Holy Communion.
Bakhita was filled with joy, she understood now that Jesus had always been there watching over her even when she did not know his name.

Bakhita wanted to love and serve Jesus in a special way so she became a sister. She cooked meals for the sisters and the children in the school. She was very popular with the children who loved to hear her stories and be with her. She died in 1947; she was happy because she knew she was going to Heaven to be with her Heavenly Father who loved her. ➤

 What do you think?

1   Can you imagine how frightened Bakhita was when she was captured? Do you have a prayer you say when you are frightened?

2   Before Bakhita heard about God she had a feeling that there was someone there with her. How do you know God is close to you?

3   If you had met Bakhita before she became a Christian, what would you have wanted to tell her about Jesus?

Josephine Bakhita

Find out more

1 Find out what the charities CAFOD or Christian Aid do for people in Africa, especially the Sudan. They have good web sites.

2 Why is slavery wrong?

3 Bakhita was always loving and kind about the people who had treated her badly. How do you feel about those who may have hurt you? It is sometimes hard to be like Bakhita?
Look up Matthew, chapter 18, verses 21 to 23.
What does Jesus say about forgiveness?

Link with the Bible

When I look at the sky, which you have made, at the moon and the stars which you set in their place,...
your greatness is seen in all the world.   Psalm 8

Do you think these words might be applied to Josephine Bakhita? Why?

Can you think of any other words from the Bible which might be appropriate?

Notes for parents and teachers

The scope of stories about more friends of Jesus

This book contains stories of saints and holy people who continued to spread the Good News of Jesus. The stories are about a range of women and men from all walks of life and cultures. Some of the stories about the people in the first millennium contain apocryphal or exaggerated incidents; this is because there was little recorded and stories were passed on orally. These stories have been included because they convey a meaning or an example of a life of love.

About saints

Not all the people in these stories have the title saint. In early days saints were declared so by the popular voice of the people and it was another way of designating a holy person. Later on and today, the title saint is only bestowed after the Church has thoroughly scrutinised the life of the person and there are some miracles attributed to them.

Children could be encouraged to reflect on all those living saints they meet among their family and friends, and to know that each of us is called and helped by Jesus to be His friend.

The purpose of this book

It is hoped that this book help will to provide some examples of lives that witness to the importance of the message of Jesus Christ. The stories are presented in a chronological order, which it is hoped will give children a sense of the history of the Church.
It starts from the early days of the beginning of Christianity, through the Middle Ages, the difficult days of the Reformation and on to the spread of religious orders in the nineteenth century.

Suggestions for use

Parents and children could read these stories together at home and think about the activities. Older children might read them on their own and follow up the activities suggested. In school they could provide a useful follow-up and extension to the religious education programme. At home the stories could be told to young children and older children could read them to each other or themselves. The activities could provide a useful link with ICT and the liturgical calendar of the Church. The stories could be linked into the teaching of history. Teachers may find the stories useful as a resource for worship.

Calendar of feast days

January	31st	John Bosco
February	1st	Brigid
	11th	Caedmon
March	1st	David
	10th	Marie Eugenie
	20th	Cuthbert
April	16th	Bernadette Soubirous
May	27th	Augustine of Canterbury
June	19th	Julian of Norwich
	20th	Alban
	22nd	Thomas More
September	17th	Hildegard of Bingham
October	1st	Josephine Bakhita
	4th	Francis of Assisi
	25th	*Feast of the English Martyrs*
		– Margaret Clitherow
		– Nicholas Owen
November	3rd	Martin de Porres
	11th	Martin of Tours
	16th	Margaret of Scotland
	18th	Hilda of Whitby
December	3rd	Francis Xavier
	6th	Nicholas
	29th	Thomas of Canterbury